D1030695

British Redcoats

by David Walsh

BELLWETHER MEDIA · MINNEAPOLIS, MN

Are you ready to take it to the extreme?
Torque books thrust you into the action-packed world
of sports, vehicles, mystery, and adventure. These books
may include dirt, smoke, fire, and dangerous stunts.
Warning: read at your own risk.

Library of Congress Cataloging-in-Publication Data

Walsh, David, 1969-
 British Redcoats / by David Walsh.
    p. cm. -- (Torque: history's greatest warriors)
 Summary: "Engaging images accompany information about British Redcoats. The combination of
high-interest subject matter and light text is intended for students in grades 3 through 7"--Provided by
publisher.
 Includes bibliographical references and index.
 ISBN 978-1-60014-627-5 (hardcover : alk. paper)
 1. Great Britain. Army--History--Juvenile literature. I. Title.
 UA649.W28 2012
 355.10941'0903--dc22   2011004936

This edition first published in 2012 by Bellwether Media, Inc.

Printed in the United States of America, North Mankato, MN.

Contents

Who Were the British Redcoats?

From the late 1700s until the early 1900s, Great Britain had the largest **empire** in the world. It included land on every continent. The British Army helped build and control this huge empire. Its soldiers were called **regulars**. They became known as Redcoats because of their bright red uniforms.

American colonists used the term "Redcoat" as an insult during the American Revolutionary War.

Redcoats were organized into **infantry regiments**. They marched from place to place. A single Redcoat was no great warrior. However, a group of Redcoats was a deadly force. Redcoats were **disciplined** and well-trained soldiers. They followed orders and stood their ground against enemy fire. Their great numbers and discipline helped them overpower almost any enemy.

British Redcoat Training

All Redcoats were volunteers. Many of them came from poor families. The army was their only way to earn money. Some were criminals who chose to join the army instead of go to prison.

New **recruits** trained for about a year. They practiced marching in **formation**. Soldiers showed them how to load and fire weapons. Recruits also mastered hand-to-hand combat.

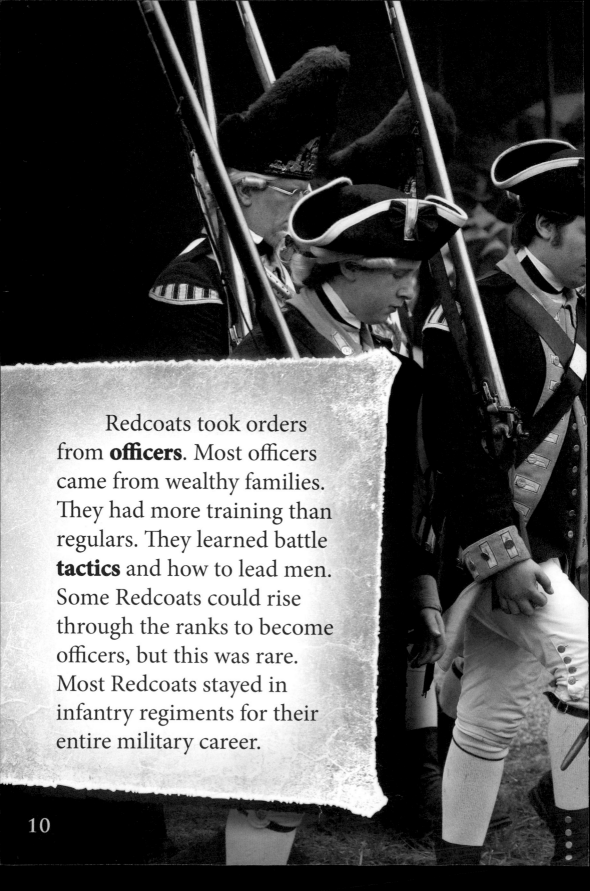

Redcoats took orders from **officers**. Most officers came from wealthy families. They had more training than regulars. They learned battle **tactics** and how to lead men. Some Redcoats could rise through the ranks to become officers, but this was rare. Most Redcoats stayed in infantry regiments for their entire military career.

All Redcoats carried **muskets**. These guns had a range of about 240 feet (73 meters). Muskets took a long time to load and were not very **accurate**. One shooter could easily miss a target. However, regiments fired hundreds of muskets at once. Few armies could stand up to a **volley** of Redcoat musket fire.

Redcoats formed two or three lines in battle. The lines would fire at different times. One line would fire while another reloaded.

A bayonet was a sharp blade attached to the end of a musket. Redcoats used bayonets in hand-to-hand combat.

Ready, Aim, Fire: Redcoat Reloading

It was important for a Redcoat to reload his musket quickly. A skilled Redcoat could reload his musket in less than 15 seconds.

hammer

flash pan

Steps to Reloading

1) Pour gunpowder into the flash pan and down the barrel

2) Put a lead ball into the barrel

3) Use the ramrod to push the ball down the barrel

4) Raise the musket and pull back the hammer

5) Aim and fire

barrel

ramrod

It was important for all Redcoats to look the same. Their red jackets showed the enemy that they were a united force. The shade of red changed over time. Early on, coats were rust-colored. Later, they were bright red. Pants, boots, and a hat completed the uniform.

No one is sure why Redcoats wore red. Some think it was to hide wounds from the enemy.

The Decline of the British Redcoats

The British lost the **American Revolutionary War** in 1783. It was a big defeat for the Redcoats and the rest of the British military. Great Britain had lost control of its North American **colonies**. However, it remained powerful in other parts of the world. The Redcoats were still a powerful military force.

The British Army still wears red today. However, it is only worn on formal occasions.

War tactics began to change in the 1800s. New guns could shoot farther and with greater accuracy. They could fire many shots without reloading. Advanced **artillery** allowed armies to attack from great distances. Redcoats could no longer line up and fire at the enemy without suffering heavy losses. They had to change their tactics. A more modern army emerged. The British Redcoats had fired their last volley.

Glossary

accurate—performing in a precise way

American Revolutionary War—a war between Great Britain and its American colonies; the colonies won the war.

artillery—firearms that shoot large objects such as cannonballs and explosives

colonies—territories owned and settled by people from another country

disciplined—showing order and control

empire—a kingdom made up of many lands

formation—a set arrangement; British Redcoats marched and fought in formations.

infantry regiments—groups of foot soldiers who fight together in land battles

muskets—guns used by British Redcoats; muskets fired large bullets, were not accurate, and took a long time to load.

officers—military members who rank above regulars; officers give orders to regulars.

recruits—people in training to join the military

regulars—soldiers in the army

tactics—military strategies

volley—a large number of bullets fired at the same time

To Learn More

AT THE LIBRARY

Anderson, Dale. *Soldiers and Sailors in the American Revolution*. Milwaukee, Wisc.: World Almanac Library, 2006.

Catel, Patrick. *Soldiers of the Revolutionary War*. Chicago, Ill.: Heinemann Library, 2011.

Weil, Ann. *British Redcoats*. Mankato, Minn.: Capstone Press, 2008.

ON THE WEB

Learning more about British Redcoats is as easy as 1, 2, 3.

1. Go to www.factsurfer.com.

2. Enter "British Redcoats" into the search box.

3. Click the "Surf" button and you will see a list of related Web sites.

With factsurfer.com, finding more information is just a click away.

Index

The images in this book are reproduced through the courtesy of: Nik Keevil/
Alamy, front cover; Mar Photographics/Alamy, pp. 4-5; North Wind Picture
Archives/Alamy, pp. 6-7; Mim Friday/Alamy, p. 9; Visions LLC/Photolibrary,
pp. 10-11; Malcolm Fairman/Alamy, p. 12; Royal Armouries/Photolibrary, pp.
14-15, 17; Lana Sundman/Alamy, p. 15; Chantal de Bruijne, p. 16; J.T. Lewis,
pp. 18-19; Barrett & MacKay/Age Fotostock, pp. 20-21.